THE
INSPIRED
ATHLETE

Risa, Teal, & Violet,

Thank you for our time together in NY! I love you all so much. keep shining your light & stay connected. much love, joy, & nothing but positive vibes for a beautiful future.

STAY INSPIRED

AARON WEXLER

—— THE ——
INSPIRED
ATHLETE

STAY INSPIRED IN & OUT OF YOUR GAME

COPYRIGHT © 2022 by Aaron Wexler

EDITOR: Tom Vater
WRITING COACH & MENTOR: Brian Gruber

PYRAMID ART by Hailey Badonivav
COVER ART by MA Rehman
AUTHOR PHOTO by Bader Howar
INTERIOR BOOK DESIGN by Alexandru Oprescu

CONTENTS

Homage and Respect to Coach John Wooden 1

Introduction 3

CHAPTER 1: LOVE 9
   Self-Love 10
   Love for Others 11
   Loving the Game 12
   Daily Practice 13
   Quotes 14

CHAPTER 2: HEALTH 17
   Overall Health 18
   Mental Health 18
   Physical Health 19
   Hydration and Electrolytes 20
   Staying Ready 21
   Daily Practice 22
   Quotes 23

CHAPTER 3: GRATITUDE AND APPRECIATION 25
   Gratitude as a Starting Point 25
   Appreciation as the Next Level 26
   Being the Energy of Appreciation 27
   Daily Practice 30
   Quotes 31

CHAPTER 4: FAMILY 33
   Daily Practice 35
   Quotes 36

CHAPTER 5: CLARITY 39
   Focus 39
   Tunnel Vision 40
   Visualization 41
   Intentional Manifesting 41
   UCLA Bruins Visualization Exercise 42
   Momentum 44
   Cutting Distraction 44
   Knowing your 'Why' 45
   Daily Practice 46
   Quotes 47

CHAPTER 6: CONFIDENCE 49
    Self Confidence.......................... 49
    No FOPO 51
    Self-Talk................................. 51
    Daily Practice 52
    Quotes 53

CHAPTER 7: CREATIVITY........................ 55
    On the Court as an Athlete 55
    On the Court as an Inspired Contributor .. 56
    Finding Joy in All You Do 57
    Daily Practice 58
    Quotes 59

CHAPTER 8: MINDFULNESS 61
    Becoming Meta-Aware....................... 61
    Mindset Expansion 62
    Growth Mindset............................ 63
    Champion Mindset 63
    Self-Talk................................. 64
    Champion Mindset Mantras.................. 64
    The Peace Sign 65
    Failure Response System 66
    Daily Practice 67
    Quotes 68

CHAPTER 9: BOLD ACTION...................... 71
    Making a Plan............................. 72
    Allow Yourself to Go for it 73
    Stay Courageous 73
    Daily Practice 76
    Quotes 77

CHAPTER 10: INSPIRED LIVING 79
    Daily Practice 81
    Quotes 82

Acknowledgements 86

Homage and Respect to Kobe Bryant.............. 87

Tribute to Mom & Dad 88

The Love Car Wash.............................. 89

My Writing Coach............................... 90

Paying it Forward 91

Contributions.................................. 93

A guidebook for athletes on how to stay inspired both in and out of their game. It includes ideas for personal growth, tools for more consistent inspiration, and motivational quotes from accomplished competitors.

Dedicated to all the athletes I have coached, and to all the coaches who have helped me on my leadership journey.

"I am happy and grateful for what I have, focused and determined for what I want."

—AARON WEXLER

"Success is peace of mind, which is a direct result of self-satisfaction in knowing you made the effort to become the best of which you are capable."

—JOHN WOODEN

Homage and Respect to Coach John Wooden

When I got the inspired nudge to write this book, I'm not going to lie, I was afraid. It seemed such a daunting task. But I made the decision to take on the challenge and try to have fun with the journey. This project has been one of the most amazing experiences of my life. I thought back to all I have gone through as an athlete, all of the inspiring people who nudged me along, and I realized that there wasn't one way to do it all, that I had to figure it out as I went along my path. What kept driving me forward was the joy I felt from practicing my craft, both as a player and a coach. But I didn't feel like that all the time. There were many years when I felt uninspired to keep going, and as I look back, I wish I had more tools to help me stay inspired more often.

John Wooden has had a huge influence in athletics and in life. Coach Wooden is a legend in the history of sports.

He won 10 national championships in 12 years as the Head Coach for the UCLA men's basketball team, including 7 in a row, as well as receiving the honor of "national coach of the year" 7 times. I've read many of his books. His famous Pyramid of Success was fixed in my mind from an early age; it was even painted on the wall outside of the gym at UCLA when I attended as a player and as a coach. Wooden's Pyramid of Success became part of my focus on a daily basis. It really helped mold a competitive mindset.

I started coaching when I was twenty years old, and quickly fell in love with it—the craft, the process, the journey, the emotions, the experiences, the upshots, as well as the relationships built. I realized early on that coaches really help to create better versions of the people they work with.

I created my own version of a principled pyramid when I was in my late 20s, heavily inspired by Wooden's original. I decided to give it out as an end-of-the-season gift to my 15u club volleyball team. I had Wooden's Pyramid of Success on one side and the Pyramid of Inspired Living, the one I had created, on the other. I wanted to make sure they knew how inspired I was by Coach Wooden's work, and I wanted them—and others—to realize that you can create your own pyramid or roadmap with your own values and unique ideas.

The purpose of the Pyramid of Inspired Living is to help athletes and coaches realize that they can be as motivated outside the game as they are inside. I'm not as accomplished or wise as the great John Wooden, but I share with him the internal commitment to help others. I give thanks to John Wooden for inspiring me, and I hope this book will inspire others. I wrote it to guide you to live an inspired life in and out of the game, but also to inspire you to pay your knowledge and blessings forward.

Introduction

THE INSPIRED ATHLETE IS THE ATHLETE I'VE ALWAYS WANTED to be, and it is the athlete who I strive to be now. It's the athlete who is unconditionally stoked on his own journey, and who loves every minute of it, no matter what the outcome of a competition might be.

The inspired athlete radiates joy and helps others to do the same.

The inspired athlete often has moments of inspiration and is aware when he's inspired both in and out of the game.

But how do we "stay inspired" on a truly consistent basis? How do we find inspiration when it's not there? For many years, I struggled to stay inspired continuously. Whether it would be internal or external factors, as an athlete, it was a challenge to constantly stay in that inspired place.

I now know that staying inspired is all about tuning out the noise and getting into a steady mental state of appreciation. Appreciation for all of it. Appreciation for each breath. Appreciation for the gift of life itself. Appreciation for each competition, and for each relationship we create along our athletic journey. When we can stay consistently in this state, the universe seems to smile back at us, as if to wink and say, "I see you, I appreciate you, and I will provide you with all your intentions and desires. I got your back."

This is all practice. Becoming limitless and powerful in your practice is a choice. It's a mindset based on the idea of 'inspired living' *and* being aligned with your true self.

No one else will choose this path for you. You must decide that this is the energetic vibration with which you are going to live your life. Living your life with inspiration means living true to your spirit, and true to your unique journey. Even the word 'inspiring' is made up from the words 'in' and 'spirit'. Inspired living is the goal, on a day-to-day, and even moment-to-moment basis. We each have our own vision of an inspired life, and it is up to us to figure out what that really means.

Throughout my years of competing both as an athlete and working as a coach, I found myself exceedingly curious about the idea of 'inspired living' and how to find that state more often. I felt that if I could practice 'staying inspired' more often, I would actually become a better athlete and a better coach, because I was constantly seeking how I could become the best version of myself.

I wrote The Inspired Athlete to help you create the best version of yourself both within and outside of your game, and help you to stay continually inspired by studying, considering, and applying the building blocks of my Pyramid of Inspired Living.

The following chapters and messages have been written to a younger version of myself, with the hope that anyone reading gains value from my thoughts to allow themselves to find inspiration in their own way.

The Inspired Athlete is not intended to be read cover to cover in one sitting. It is meant to be picked up throughout the day, for ideas to be considered and put into action. The more you are thinking, acting, and interacting with others from a place of inspiration, the better you feel, and the better your experiences and achievements. It can even help you find the 'flow' state.

'Inspired Living' is a practice, a choice, a way of living life to its fullest potential, a way to practice your own alignment to the divine energy that is in us and around us, a pathway to be as in tune with your inner being or true self as possible. It's about respecting this journey of mind-body-soul alignment so much that we commit to reconditioning our minds and training our thought processes to reflect our true inner power. It's about lifting up those around us, attracting positive energy in others, and being a magnet for greatness. It's about inspiring others around us to be great.

It's about always staying a humble student, and always doing our best to listen, to allow your inner power to guide us. The more we recognize this innate power in all of us, the more we operate from a place of gratitude, inspiration, and creativity, which leads to a life filled with joy, greatness, fulfillment, and impact. I believe that this should be a focus for everyone's legacy, because this is how we can create a positive impact on others and to try to leave the world in a better state than when we found it. I believe this is one of the reasons why we are here.

The Pyramid of Inspired Living provides tools to practice this way of living each moment with a feeling of alignment.

Throughout the journey of writing this book, I interviewed people living their versions of an inspired life. I have met with coaches, Olympic champions, trainers, successful business owners, spiritual leaders, authors, podcasters, influencers, and friends. I am inspired by what I have learned by my interactions with all of them. I gained the wisdom that while it's one thing to be inspired in your craft, it's an altogether different game when you inspire someone else.

"The most important thing is to try and inspire people, so that they can be great in whatever they want to do."

—KOBE BRYANT

The following chapters provide a look into the principles of the building blocks of the Pyramid of Inspired Living. Each represents an aspect of thinking, acting, and creating from a place of inspiration. You will learn how to draw thoughts from a place of deep personal motivation, so that your actions will be aligned with what you are here to accomplish, both in and out of your game.

I have added quotes from many of the guests I have interviewed on my podcast, and I am happy to share their wisdom and knowledge on these pages.

I want to be clear that I am not directing you on how you should live your life! These are merely insights and reflections to help you remember who you really are, what you really want, where you really want to go, designed to help you become the best version of yourself more often.

The Pyramid of Inspired Living is inspired by the Pyramid of Success, developed by John Wooden. When I was at UCLA, I saw the Pyramid of Success every day. While I like it and appreciate it, the top of it—Competitive Greatness—always made me think. While I am a competitor, and I resonate with the idea of competitive greatness, it's not at the top of my pyramid.

'Inspired Living', in and out of the game, is.

What does that really mean? How do we get inspired when we are not? How do we maintain that feeling when we are? What action steps can we take to get there quicker and more often?

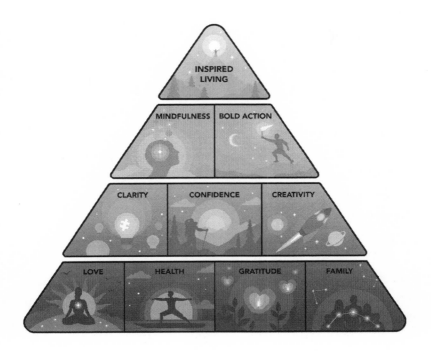

1

Love

WHEN I DECIDED THAT I WAS GOING TO WRITE A BOOK about 'staying inspired', my mind immediately turned to the feeling of love—self-love, love for the game, love for the journey itself, love for the victories, challenges, and relationships made along the way, for finding the joy in all of it. I remember once hearing or reading about how the legendary coach Wooden regretted that he left out the word 'love' from his Pyramid of Success, and that helped inspire me to make it the cornerstone and foundational value of the Pyramid of Inspired Living.

Love is one of those things that we don't really talk about or think about, it's more something we feel. When you really think about it, it's the most important thing for all of us, because, at the end of the day, that is what we all want: to love and to be loved.

Finding the joy of it all is allowing yourself to fall in love with the journey. We must all find what we love and pursue that thing, because that is the first step on a path to staying inspired and living a life full of inspiration.

This includes self-love, love for the game, love for the ability to compete, and love for everyone you meet along the way. You must find love even in the hard days, the injuries and losses, the setbacks and challenges, because these can ultimately make you stronger.

Self-Love

As a young athlete, I remember laughing at the idea of self-love. I had heard about it, read about it, and even thought about it a little, but it wasn't until very recently that I began to understand the true value of loving yourself first before anything else. Without this step, you may get stuck in an endless cycle of comparing yourself to others. Avoiding exactly this is one of the main concepts of this book.

For me, self-love includes raising my energetic vibration on a daily basis through meditation, listening to inspiring people on podcasts, and connecting with others in a mindful way. It's remembering who I really am, what I really want, and how I really want to feel—energetically calibrating to these things before I take any action. Self-love is also about forgiving yourself for past mistakes.

Love for Others

Love is the cornerstone of life itself. It is the most important building block in the Pyramid of Inspired Living. There's no age difference or time difference in love. Love radiates in us and around us at all times, and like energy, cannot be created or destroyed. Love is the deepest emotion we can have! Starting from a mindset of love in all that we do is the goal, which will allow us to feel more confident—coming from a place of love rather than fear.

Unconditional Love is the next level. It literally means that the conditions around us don't matter more than the love we innately have inside us all. It's remembering that the conditions we are currently experiencing are guaranteed to change since change is the only constant, and knowing that we can practice unconditional love in every moment. Self-love, love for others, and love for our craft can be unconditional.

There is a clear difference in outcomes if we *first* choose to operate from a place of love. That difference can be felt and especially noticed during our performance on the court, on the field, in school, in business, in relationships, or anytime we are practicing our craft. Tell everyone in your life who you love that you love them. Don't hesitate. Do not wait for holidays or certain dates on the calendar to express your love. Do not judge love as a too-precious type of word or emotion to share.

Loving the Game

I remember falling in love with sports at a very early age. Tennis was my first love. On weekends, I used to play tennis with my dad Howard and grandfather Sy, at the Mulholland Tennis Club in Los Angeles, and I distinctly remember absolutely loving learning the hitting technique, the journey of getting better, and the thrill of competing. My next love of sports was baseball. My dad and I used to play catch for hours on our front lawn or at Penmar Park in Venice and I absolutely loved it. I soon after found beach volleyball and absolutely fell in love with that too and ran with it. I'm so grateful for this, because it helped me get into college, travel the world, and become an entrepreneur.

I loved the process of falling in love with sports and still do. Every minute of it. The triumphs, the challenges, the setbacks, the learning, the growth, but especially the people I connected with and the relationships I created along my journey. Mark Ozzello, my first coach, was a great influence on learning how to coach. He told me my teams "will never remember the scores, but they will always remember you".

One thing I have done is to 'personify' the game, asking the game questions, like, what more can I do for you? What more do you want from me? How can I share you with others and have them love you too?

Get comfortable with the idea of love, especially self-love—you have to love yourself first! You must love yourself and your life and your journey.

DAILY PRACTICE

» *Ask yourself: What areas of my life deserve more love? This could be with yourself, your family, your game, your training, or anything else that could use more love.*

» *Make a list of everything about your sport and your game that you love. Keep this list someplace that you see it every day and add to it over time.*

» *Reach out to someone who might not be expecting to hear from you and tell them that you love them. Start with one person, and as this becomes less 'weird', tell more people. There should be nothing weird about expressing your love.*

» *Surround yourself with people who radiate love.*

QUOTES

"In my playing days, I'd be frustrated and not play as well as I wanted. Then I look around and I think, oh my god, I'm playing a game I love, doing something I love. How lucky am I to have this opportunity?"

—MARI-JO DEUTSCHMAN,
COACH & MENTOR

"I am an athlete who sincerely loves training. And joy to me is the feeling of progress. And where I feel my progress is, is in my training. I love working hard. I love being sharpened, and all these things. And so, when it comes time to enter the arena, to me if I've done that right, I was consistent, I gave everything I had, I was aligned with my partner. I showed up, you know, with kindness and sincerity. I gave 100%."

—KERRI WALSH JENNINGS,
3X OLYMPIC GOLD MEDALIST, 5X OLYMPIAN

"I try to be positive, and I know a lot of people are mad and frustrated and negative, but I really think love heals everything, and as long as we just keep feeding what is positive, we can be better for the next generation. And they have to do better than what we're doing."

—ANTHONY DAVIS,
STATE CHAMPION BASKETBALL COACH

"So, fear of people's opinions. I think it's a great constructor of potential and so how do you deal with it? I think it comes from a place of love. I love you and I don't, I don't care what you think of me."

—DR. MICHAEL GERVAIS,
SPORT PSYCHOLOGIST WHO HELPED THE INAUGURAL
USA SURFING TEAM TO A GOLD MEDAL AT THE 2020 TOKYO OLYMPICS

"I put in the work. I got to this point. I showed up every day and I practiced. And I'm going to just trust that that was enough because I set my intention every day in practice. I trust myself and I trust the skills I've developed to get here. And I don't need to do anything else. And when I've done practice, like, that's how I like to think of the game. I think you inspire yourself in that game because you're like, wow, I made it here. I made it to this game. I went through all those grueling practices month after month. And now I'm here and I'm just going to trust what I'm just going to do, what I've always done, and I don't need to be anyone else in myself during the game."

—LILY JUSTINE,
2X NCAA CHAMPION AT UCLA

"The best thing you can do is just love on people and not be scared to tell people that, and sometimes it makes people really uncomfortable, but I will. That almost makes me like it even more."

—CAMRYN IRWIN, SPORTS BROADCASTER
FOR AVP & SUPER BOWL CHAMPIONS LA RAMS

2

Health

THERE IS ABSOLUTELY NOTHING BETTER IN THE WHOLE world than feeling good! Mentally, physically, and emotionally. Your own health is your first priority over everything. True health is the process of finding the path of least resistance to your true self, your inner self, and listening to what it needs, because it will tell you.

The healthier you are, the more clearly you will hear your inner self guide you. If you listen carefully, it will lead you on a journey of respecting your physical body enough to always make the effort to be in the best shape of your life.

Overall Health

Taking care of yourself is your number one job, your number one priority, and it takes daily commitment. Learn what your body needs to achieve excellent health. Create positive habits for yourself that are nurturing and healthy.

Get good sleep. Drink plenty of water. Make balanced nutritional choices, and always think about how you'll feel after you eat something before you eat it. Say no to things that don't serve the best version of you.

Our bodies are our homes. They change daily and need and deserve constant appreciation and attention. Pain is the first sign of an imbalance, so accommodate pain with healing modalities, positive thoughts, and appropriate actions.

Learn about how your body best functions and moves. Learn about your kinetic chain and know that not only can you heal from injury, but you can come back stronger than you were before your injury.

Mental Health

Mental Health is about making sure you are in a positive mental place. It's about being authentic, vulnerable, and calm. It's about being honest with yourself as well as others and never comparing yourself to others. It's about respecting your own needs, listening to your intuition and staying in positive self-talk (which we will get into more later). It's also about asking for help when you are at your most vulnerable.

Mental health is also about knowing when to rest. Many athletes want to push ourselves to the brink of exhaustion, and while there is great value in hard work, getting enough rest to be fully recharged for the next day is just as important.

Physical Health

I've been through many injuries throughout my career, but two stick out, especially for how they impacted me and my life and the message I want to share.

During my freshman year at UCLA, I was doing an Olympic level jump training sequence in the UCLA basement athlete weight room with Jeff Nygard, who was an assistant coach at the time. It was a series of different plyometric moves—over hurdles, on top of different-sized jump boxes, lateral jumps, and controlled landings. I was stoked to be working out with an Olympian and my ego kept telling me I could keep up with his workout. I did the whole workout with him, and on the very last landing, I felt a tweak in my knee. I then got an MRI and found out I had a medial meniscus tear in my right knee and was immediately scheduled for surgery.

Four years later as a senior during a practice, I experienced the exact same injury, except this time it was on my left knee after a quick lateral move. I was soon thereafter scheduled for surgery, again.

The reason that I am sharing these two injuries is that I now know that not only are they very preventable with proper body mechanics awareness, but with the right knowledge and programming, injuries can actually make you stronger in the long run. They force you to learn about how your body works, (though you should not wait for an injury to learn biomechanics) and they can help you have more efficient movement in the long run. These injuries made me understand the following:

1. Having awareness of how your body works is essential
2. Being mindful of your posture at all times is essential
3. Pain is a key indicator that something needs more attention

4. A thorough planned training regimen designed by a fitness professional is imperative
5. Weight training techniques ought to be taught and learned at an early age, prior to adding more weight
6. Balance, flexibility, and core strength training are vital at every stage in the athlete's journey

Hydration and Electrolytes

In 2009, I went down bad with severe muscle cramps at The Manhattan Beach Open Qualifier. Gray Garrett and I had just beaten legends Scott Ayakatubby and Brent Frohoff in a barn burner three-set match in front of a hostile crowd heavily rooting for the other guys and heckling us at every point. I remember being so pumped for beating them, yet also so tired. I remember walking up to the local grocery store right after the match to get more water, and on my way back I heard our names called for the next match, the one leading to the main draw. With just a few minutes of rest, on a hot summer day, my body started to cramp in the first game. I had never experienced full-body cramping. Wow! What pain! It started in my feet, and gradually went up my legs with increasing intensity. I took a medical timeout and tried to drink a lot of Gatorade and eat bananas so I could keep going, but after a few ensuing points, my body locked up and I realized I couldn't go on. I was carted off to the medical tent with intense full body cramps. The AVP doctors hooked me up to an IV. I was in a full body shake. It felt like an uncontrollable seizure, and it was scary. The doctors called an ambulance because they were not exactly sure what was happening to me. Two "banana bags" later, my body calmed down and I was able to leave with my dad under my own power, but I did have to forfeit that match. This was a huge disappointment and low moment for me in my athletic career. I felt discouraged, embarrassed, and I felt like I let myself as well as Gray, my teammate, down.

Leading up to this incident, I felt prepared with my nutrition and hydration, but obviously I had missed something. I went to get bloodwork—it came back normal. The diagnosis was one of two things: Either I had been severely dehydrated, or I had been over-hydrated enough to flush the salts out of my body.

Ever since then, I have made it a priority to make sure I am on top of my own hydration. Not only do I drink a lot of water every day, including first thing in the morning and last thing before bed, but I also include a specific electrolyte supplement into my routine. The main product I use is called *Biosteel*, and thanks to my trainer and long-time doctor, Dr. Chad Moreau, I use this product almost every day. It contains balanced electrolytes, amino acids and no sugar.

Whatever stage in your athletic journey, make sure you are supplementing your water intake with electrolytes. Coconut water is a great way to naturally hydrate, and I also recommend a natural product called *Recharge* and a product called *Liquid IV*.

Staying Ready

Move! Your body wants you to move it, especially on your off days. Light movement on your rest days is essential.

Committing to a personalized, periodized training program based on upcoming competitions is the best way to reach your fitness goals and to always 'stay ready so you don't have to get ready'. This includes training and nutrition. Find a professional trainer and nutritionist who can help you stay accountable to your needs and goals.

DAILY PRACTICE

» *Drink more water, tell yourself you are strong and healthy, and breathe deep throughout the day.*

» *Make time for yourself. Thank your body for being the masterpiece it is. If you have any areas of concern, thank those areas for making your inner being aware of them, and send good energy to those areas.*

» *Keep your nutritional choices smart and healthy.*

QUOTES

"At the cornerstone of everything is just how healthy I feel, right? It's how well I sleep, it's how well I recover. And then ultimately, how much energy and how clear I am as it relates to the decisions that I need to make to continually push my evolution towards my ideal life forward, right."

—**ROB DYRDEK**, FORMER PRO SKATEBOARDER, ENTREPRENEUR, HOST OF RIDICULOUSNESS & BUILD WITH ROB PODCAST

"You know, rest is great, it's important. Breathing is up there at the top, it's profoundly important and definitely can help with anxiety immensely, and especially in this pandemic, I mean, you want to talk about dealing with anxiety, but breathwork *is all about reducing anxiety and, I think we have a natural connection to the importance of breathing because we deal with being in the ocean and so we always have that on our mind but yeah, there's just no one that doesn't benefit from it and athletes, and I mean we do a lot of work around breathing in through the nose for cardio training as well as biking, running, you know, rowing assault with all this breathing stuff. I mean, there's so many different patterns that you can do. But the nose is the most important, you know, the nose is the king."*

—**LAIRD HAMILTON**, LEGENDARY BIG WAVE SURFER & ENTREPRENEUR

"I don't need to learn the lesson that my health is important. I get it. I understand it. That's why I'm passionate about health, not because I'm like, let's have six pack abs. It's one of the greatest gifts, besides your friends and family, is your health."

—**GABBY REECE**, FORMER PRO BEACH VOLLEYBALL PLAYER, FITNESS ENTHUSIAST, PODCAST HOST

"Getting yourself just to move in a situation where you don't want to move is oftentimes all it takes and then you kind of get into it. To that piece, if you can just get yourself to you know, hey, this is something that's gonna make me 1% better today and just get yourself to start it. It usually kicks in."

—**RICH LAMBOURNE**, OLYMPIC GOLD MEDALIST

"The biggest challenge was the autoimmune disease, for sure. It was the biggest challenge and also the biggest breakthrough for me because I feel like I tried to go through it. I didn't try to go around the problem. I went right through it. And I gained all that energy that it was trying to suck out of me. I feel like I absorbed it. And I used it and now I'm using all that same energy to go in the right direction."

—**TRI BOURNE**, OLYMPIAN & 5X AVP CHAMPION

"This mindful breathing you're trying to get when you are calm, and you're not panting. That's when you play your best."

—**ERIC FONOIMOANA**,
OLYMPIC GOLD MEDALIST & 13X AVP CHAMPION

"If this current health crisis has taught us anything, I hope it's that we need to be proactive with our health. This could bring about a new generation of health conscious people that now realize that the choices they make with regards to nutrition, exercise, sleep, and social interaction can help ensure their ability to survive and thrive."

—**DR. CHAD MOREAU**, CHIROPRACTOR, PERFORMANCE COACH,
INJURY REHAB SPECIALIST (AND MY PERSONAL TRAINER!)

CHAPTER 3

Gratitude and Appreciation

Gratitude as a Starting Point

I have found that being grateful is the best starting point for everything I want to accomplish and who I want to be in my life. It's all a gift. All of it. This is the mindset of someone who radiates gratitude, and often follows the energy of love.

The idea of gratitude is simply becoming aware that everything is a gift and it's all for you. It's a mindset that creates happiness, which leads to inspired action. Being grateful for everything in our lives—people, experiences, your own body and mind, material things, wins, losses, successes, failures, ups and downs-everything. Everything is learning, and every moment is an opportunity for our spirit to learn and grow. Even when we are challenged, we should be thinking, 'I'm so grateful I have an opportunity to work through this'.

Being grateful is a choice, since we have the option to be in love or fear at every moment. In all situations, choose to start from love and gratitude, and go from there.

Appreciation as the Next Level

The next step to really allowing the idea of gratitude to be applied in your life is appreciation. When you appreciate someone or something, you are not just grateful for that person or thing. You are being exponentially grateful for it. Radiate appreciation all day long, and let your attitude always be founded in a place of appreciation.

Every time I sat down to work on this project, I got into a deep place of gratitude and appreciation first. I thought, 'I am so grateful to have a project to work on that could potentially create enormous ripples of positive impact around the world forever'.

Take that energy into all that you do.

Some of the most successful people I have met seem to be innately grateful for their success. Legendary volleyball coach (Crossroads School), mentor, and dear friend Mari Jo Deutschman radiates happiness and gratitude, and it's one of the first things you feel when meeting her. Olympic champion and friend Dain Blanton also operates from a place of appreciation first. You can sense it. Sometimes it doesn't take words, it's more of an energy they give off.

There are some moments in life where you may feel overjoyed with gratitude. On a recent solo trip to Koh Phangan Thailand, I remember this feeling so strongly as I sat in the airport waiting for my flight home. I thought of all the time and mind power I had spent manifesting and preparing for this trip, all the people that had made it possible for me, all the people I met, and all the experiences I was able to have. As I sat there, I really allowed myself to feel the deep emotion of gratitude for it all, and it felt so good! I cried tears of pure joy, knowing that not only did I manifest such a trip, but it became crystal clear to me that the universe co-created it with me.

Being the Energy of Appreciation

When you start your training sessions, practices, and business meetings with a moment of gratitude, it tends to set the tone for a great, more productive session. This also creates humility. Be thankful for the opportunity in front of you. I find that when I stay grateful and appreciative throughout my training and coaching sessions, thankful for the chance to be successful, especially when it gets really hard, I'm able to push through better and I end up performing better.

I remember being at a low point in my life after I graduated from UCLA. I went to live with my parents to save money, to figure everything out, and to chase my dream of playing on the AVP. I tried to save up as much money as I could for traveling and for paying my trainer, by getting a job at Duke's Malibu as a busboy, bar back, and server. I was also working for my friend Dane Pearson's catering company GreatDane Catering & Events, working various functions and bartending gigs, and I would go from my parents' home in Venice to Hermosa Beach or Santa Monica, and then drive fast to make it in time for my shift at Duke's Malibu, or at a catering event. I made ok money, enough to pay my trainer, coach, and save a little for travel.

Chasing the dream of being a professional athlete was awesome. The practices, the workouts, even the job, all of that was great. But every once in a while, I didn't feel like doing anything. I felt uninspired. I felt flat and over it all. Those were the days I just sat there and felt sorry for myself. Those were the days I compared myself to others. Those were the days I questioned myself and my dreams and allowed that feeling of indecision to dominate me.

After a while, I had enough of all that. I had been asked to coach kids at a local club, and I took that gig over working at the restaurant. It was during my new coaching gig when my friend Karl Owens and I began regularly meeting up at a place in Santa Monica near the beach and began openly expressing our gratitude to each other—for anything that we could come up with for that particular day. We started vocalizing what we were grateful for in our lives on that particular day, and we made a consistent habit out of this practice. It felt weird and cheesy at first, but at the end of every session it always felt so good. It felt good to be vulnerable and to share what was going on in our lives. It felt good to listen and to hold space for each other. It felt really good to put attention to and to focus on what we were grateful for in our lives. Most of the time, that was our health, our family, and something about progress in our personal and professional lives.

Soon thereafter, we created gratitude circles. We would invite a few friends to meet to do these gratitude shares, because we knew how powerful these meetups were for us, so we wanted to share that feeling with others.

I remember thinking that the idea of gratitude was the 'salt of the earth'. It had a hand in creating everything and helped to make everyone ready for more. It's an acknowledgment of the beauty and power of what has already manifested and of what's coming next. Feeling it is the first level and expressing it out loud helps turn it into appreciation. Appreciation is honoring the gratitude you have for something or someone and leveling that up with more honor.

Shortly after the gratitude circles became regular events, I set up my business as WestCoast Beach Volleyball Club, with my best friend Travis Schoonover, auspiciously very close to the same gratitude meeting spot. We made it a priority to teach young athletes the concepts of gratitude and appreciation and let those ideas permeate into the culture of our business. I'm soooo grateful that after our start in 2013, we have enjoyed 9+ years of our ever growing Club!

DAILY PRACTICE

» *List out: Who, what, when, where, and why are you grateful today? What specific event recently happened in your life that you're grateful for? The more you practice this, the more you will radiate gratitude and appreciation.*

» *Meet up with someone and create a gratitude circle. Do a social media post or journal about what it is that you're grateful for. Reach out to someone who is not expecting to hear from you and tell them that you're grateful for them.*

» *Ask others what they are grateful for and what inspires them—even if it's out of the blue.*

QUOTES

"So, productivity is the second lens and then the lens of gratitude, which is the most powerful, because that lens of gratitude will help you find the light, the love and the lessons in every single thing that you do, no matter what the exterior circumstances are."

—**DAVID MELTZER**, SPORTS AGENT, ENTREPRENEUR, AUTHOR, PODCAST HOST

"Man, gratitude, that's, that's the key. That is the key. Yeah, I was specifically told by one of the monks, that was a key."

—**PRINCE DANIELS JR.**, FORMER NFL RUNNING BACK, RESILIENCE TRAINER & SELF ACTUALIZATION STRATEGIST

"I think being inspired by things was always a skill, but finding them in different places that I didn't initially find them in became a skill that I had to, like, develop. Yeah, find them in ways and in scenarios that normally I wouldn't have paid attention to. Right. Um, that definitely was a skill

that I acquired. Yes, just through living life and, and experiencing other things and appreciating those things that slowly developed and got better and better. So that you were able to really appreciate anyone in anything they do and find something that's inspiring."

—**CASEY PATTERSON**, OLYMPIAN & 18X AVP CHAMPION

"And you just really have to be grateful. For me framing stuff that like hey, like, step back, what I'm doing is really cool. And it is a gift. And whatever small inconvenience I find in the big picture is just so trivial. I should be grateful."

—BILLY ALLEN, 2X AVP CHAMPION

"I think that the sport of volleyball and being part of a team, and there are so many lessons that, you know, not that you take for granted, because I didn't, but that certain things, you know, until the moment you're like, wow, I just really am grateful for those experiences and opportunities that seemed very, like, specific in the moment for what we were doing. But really, it's these life lessons that are always valuable and are so helpful."

—GIGI HADID,
SUPERMODEL & FORMER VOLLEYBALL PLAYER

"Success to me is the opportunity to be, and learn from others, and if you can see it, and it's the path that you want, and you can go after it, that could be defined as success. Certainly, I feel just a ton of gratitude and I am fortunate that there was a path towards what I was passionate about doing for a living and doing it at a high level."

—STEIN METZGER OLYMPIAN, 16X AVP CHAMPION,
3X NCAA CHAMPION, BACK TO BACK NCAA CHAMPION AS HEAD COACH

"I believe that the present moment is very, very important. And it's very powerful. And you should be grateful for every single moment that we have, because you could be gone tomorrow. You know, if you have health, have gratitude for health, if you have a roof over your head, have gratitude for that, if you have friends, have gratitude for that people love you, gratitude for everything. Whatever you have going for you, just be very grateful. And cherish every moment."

—TIMOTHY SCHULTZ, POWERBALL WINNER

AARON WEXLER

CHAPTER

4

Family

BEFORE I STARTED THIS PROJECT, I WAS GOING THROUGH a tough time with my family. Changes were taking place, we were fighting a lot, and we even had group therapy sessions together. We weren't all on the same page. As I got deeper into this project, I realized how lucky I was to have a beautiful loving family who I could talk to everyday, who I could inspire and they could inspire me, and who would always be there for me and I for them, no matter what.

There is a spiritual school of thought that we chose our parents, and we all knew what we were getting ourselves into before choosing to enter this physical manifestation. Whether or not that is what you believe, love your family unconditionally and keep them very close to you, no matter what.

Even when you are mad at them, or they are mad at you, it's important to choose LOVE over FEAR. When adversity comes into your life regarding your family, finding a way to be grateful for that contrast may allow you to take the lesson from it and hopefully, the entire family may grow stronger.

Family support for your athletic journey is everything. I have so much appreciation for my parents, Howard and Evone, who supported me fully and who continue to support me on my path. It takes the journey to the next level when you can make your parents proud and let them share the emotions of winning and losing.

Sometimes, it helps to 'play for' someone in your family. When you decide to play for someone other than yourself, it can motivate you even more. Dedicate an upcoming practice or competition to 'playing for' someone in your family.

As you grow as a person and start to take flight, you may notice others in your family or even your friends being stuck. It is not your job to get other people 'unstuck'. It's better to inspire them with your own energy and actions to help them break out of old mindsets so they too can spread their wings.

Love and support family unconditionally through their challenges, and remind them how beautiful, great and divine we all are. Keep your family very close to you no matter what. Even if there have been bad vibes in the past, find a way to forgive and move forward.

DAILY PRACTICE

» *Reach out to a family member you haven't talked to in a long time to check in on them and to tell them how much you love them!*

» *Make a surprise visit to a family member who is not expecting you, for no other reason than to say hello and to connect.*

QUOTES

"I get my inspiration from my family understanding that I always wanted to, to make my family proud of me. That's where I think the source of my inspiration comes from. I never wanted to disappoint my family. That was just who I was."

—**KENNY LOFTON**, LEGENDARY MLB PLAYER

"It all starts with your parents. The inspired life was to have those guys train me, teach me, with love, they never yelled, no physicality and taught me and my sisters and brother how to communicate with others, with love."

—**MARK OSELLO**, COACH/MENTOR

 *"Your family. Those people are the ones that are gonna always be proud, no matter what you do."*

—**BRANDIE WILKERSON**,
OLYMPIAN, 3X WORLD TOUR CHAMPION

AARON WEXLER

"There's your little 'why', which is, you know, while you're playing the sport, which is part of the winter game, or get a trophy, or play with your boys, or whatever it is, but then there's a big 'why'. And in most cases, if you're an athlete, you're trying to become a professional athlete, or you are a professional athlete. And the reason you're trying to do that, is, at least in my case, personally, my big 'why' was always to make sure my family was okay. Like, I don't feel like practicing today. But is that an excuse to give up on my family because especially in the NFL, like you have one bad practice that could very well be the straw that broke the camel's back, and you're gone, you don't have the opportunity to have a bad day, or a bad play or string of bad plays. So, forget if you did have bad plays, show that you're coachable, take the coaching and move on. As long as you keep that big 'why'. Right for me, it was my family. So, I don't have an excuse to really have a bad day, and if I do, let me redirect this energy to be more productive with it. You know, and keep in mind, the fan is on your back. Right? Be the CEO of your last name."

—**GARRY GILLIAM**, JR. NFL PLAYER, CEO OF THE BRIDGE

"Well, I think I'm more inspired outside of volleyball with my family. Volleyball has been huge for me because it's given me more time than most people to spend with their families. My favorite thing to do is hang out with my wife, my kids. You know, I started coaching now. And I miss my kids when they get home from school, I'm leaving. So, if you know, that's something I gotta get through because for years and years, I was able to pick them up from school, drop them off at school, you know, do all this stuff with my family. So, I think they inspire me, you know, they love being at the tournaments. I'm just inspired by my family, and I think I bring that to the court."

—**JOHN HYDEN**, 2X OLYMPIAN, 28X AVP CHAMPION

5

Clarity

Focus

There was a time in my life when I was unclear about what I wanted. I was unclear of how to go on as an athlete, and I was unclear of my goals. I always used specific goals as an athlete, so when I experienced this lack of clarity, I was confused. It was after college, and I didn't know what I was supposed to do, and I was unsure about my own path in beach volleyball. I moved back to my parents' place in Venice and was really unmotivated, mostly because of how much uncertainty there was in the AVP schedule and pro beach volleyball tour that year. It took me some time to find clarity in how to best move forward with training, competing, and starting my business.

I also remember being really unclear after being fired from a coaching job in the middle of the season. That night I questioned my own clear path forward and realized that I had to work on my clarity and redefine my goals. In hindsight, being let go was a gift. Being unclear about who you are becoming and what you want is really frustrating, especially as an athlete. Being unclear also makes the clarity you eventually reach absolutely awesome and liberating.

So how do we find that clarity?

And once we do get that clarity, how do we allow ourselves to focus?

Tunnel Vision

Just before the 2021 Tokyo Olympics, I enjoyed the opportunity to help train the A team, April Ross and Alix Klineman, with friend and AVP Champion, Ty Tramblie. They were so focused and dialed in. They were clear about what they wanted and how they were going to get there. This was true 'tunnel vision'. They had so much clarity during those training sessions, and that clarity paid off with them going undefeated in the Olympics and winning the gold medal.

I've trained with many people over the years, both men and women, and there have been few times when I have felt that type of intense clarity and focus. Another player that comes to mind is John Hyden, a 2-time Olympian in indoor volleyball for team USA as an outside hitter, and is the oldest player to ever win a pro beach volleyball tournament. He was and still is meticulous and super-focused about his training which stems from how clear he is in his pursuit of being his best. It really helps to fine tune your own clarity when you are around other people who have that super clear clarity.

Visualization

Being clear about what you want and who you want to be will allow you to set forth on a path of becoming the best version of yourself in and out of your game. This clarity starts with learning how to quiet the mind and strengthen our intuitive voice.

As you come to know better what you want to accomplish, you begin to create visualizations of the desired outcome: winning, experiencing a joyous feeling, having a great performance, or being fully satisfied that you did your best. The most important part of visualizing is attaching desired emotion to the pictures and movies you create during visualization.

For many athletes, the emotion of 'Yes!' is a great one to focus on. What brings you this feeling!? Usually it stems from three things: A great play, a great practice session, a great match. This comes from being clear first.

Conscious visualization is a huge part of being successful. Close your eyes and see yourself winning. See yourself performing with grace and perfect technique. Attach emotion to these visuals and feel the feeling of the desired outcome. Feel how good it feels to win. Practice celebrating in your mind first, and practice visualizing success in the classroom, or in business.

Intentional Manifesting

We are manifesting all the time, whether we know it or not. Your mind is so powerful!

A great, practical way to think about how to manifest is to understand the TAR principle. Thoughts + Actions = Results.

Manifesting is simply getting extremely clear with your thoughts, and then taking the necessary action steps that reflect the intentions of your thoughts.

Then, allow it to happen.

When I was a player at UCLA, I did a visualization exercise with a hypnotist. The exercise was to lie down, focus on your breathing, and become very still and calm. As you become more and more relaxed, you start to see the best version of yourself—the person you intend to become enters the room and stands there gazing at you. This person is the ideal you, the you that you are working to become. What are some of the qualities of this person? What does she/he look like? What kind of characteristics and attributes does this person have? What kind of energy does this person have? This exercise is sort of like looking at yourself in the mirror, but the person looking back at you is the future best version of yourself. This is a great step in the journey of staying inspired.

Having true clarity is also about having a clear 'intent of purpose'. It's all about knowing what you want and allowing yourself to go for it!

UCLA Bruins Visualization Exercise

When I was a volunteer assistant for the 2011 UCLA Women's Volleyball team under head coach Mike Sealy, I created a visualization exercise with the intention of optimizing the team's success. At the time I was reading "Creative Visualization", by Shakti Gawain, which teaches how to practice visualization in a practical and fun way. I was inspired by the techniques in the book to create a ten-minute pre-practice visualization specifically for volleyball, and after typing the whole thing out I showed it to coach Sealy and asked if I could share it with the team. He gave me the green light and I led the exercise with the team before practice on the racquetball court floor. The exercise included really getting in touch with your breath first, then creating a movie theater in your mind where you project the pictures of your desired outcomes. It was here in this movie theater where we then went through all of the individual mechanics and techniques of volleyball. We would spend time seeing/hearing/feeling what the perfect techniques were like, and then spend more time celebrating winning points. That day, we had the best practice of the year and the coach asked me to lead the same visualization at an upcoming match at Cal. We went on to win that match convincingly, and for the rest of the season we continued with that visualization exercise. The team went on to win the Division 1 NCAA championship that year.

I coached varsity volleyball for Crossroads School for Arts & Science for five years. We used this same visualization technique which helped us win the school's first ever CIF championship, as well as a state regional championship and a state finals appearance.

On my *Within the Game* podcast, Dr. Mike Gervais talks about FOPO and how it can be a dangerous driving factor. FOPO, he said, is 'Fear of Other People's Opinions'. There is also something called FOMO—'Fear of Missing Out'. The more clarity you have of who you are growing into and what it is that you want to accomplish, the less FOPO and FOMO you will experience.

Momentum

How do you get clear if you are stuck?

Feeling stuck is not a great situation to be in, but it's very common. We all find ourselves stuck every now and then. Becoming unstuck is all about creating momentum on positive things and creating wins for yourself.

For athletes, it can be fun to 'gamify' your day. Find wins throughout the day. They can be small wins like making your bed in the morning, cleaning the kitchen, finishing assignments, speaking with loved ones.

Creating mini wins throughout the day is a great way to become unstuck.

Cutting Distraction

In today's world, attention is becoming a currency. Where you put your attention is so important. I like to think of your attention as your flashlight and you get to decide where to shine it, how bright, wide, or narrow you want it to be.

Meditation is one of the best tools for increasing clarity and control of your flashlight. It really helps me, especially when I do it in the morning for ten to fifteen minutes. I notice that on the days I meditate, everything seems to flow better, and my thoughts are more productive. I have found that trying too hard to quiet the mind can actually make me anxious, so I am working on allowing my mind to be still and just observing the thoughts that come. It's a challenge to stay consistent with this practice, but I have noticed that practicing meditation makes it easier for me to control my attention and to cut out distractions—anything that does not serve my greatest good.

Knowing your 'Why'

Why are you doing what you're doing? Why are you working so hard? Why are you sacrificing so much? Is it for yourself or is it for someone else?

Knowing your 'Why' is so important, because it drives you in all that you do. The more understanding you have of your own 'why', the more confident you will be in your pursuit. This is a great thing to think about and to know before you enter a training session, practice, or game. It doesn't have to be some grandiose philosophical idea; it could be as simple as 'my 'why' is to be the best version of myself as an athlete today.'

If your 'why' ever becomes unclear, spend some time getting clear on it because otherwise it can leave you in limbo.

When you understand your 'why', your intuition speaks to you loud and clear. This is your gut instinct and the voice of your innate inner power. Most of the time, this is your true self or inner being trying to express itself. It's up to you to choose to listen.

The more clarity you find with this intuitive intelligent nudge, the more clarity you will find in your thoughts, actions, and reactions. Usually if we are unclear about something, it's either because we haven't trained ourselves to listen to our own intuition, or because we are choosing to ignore it. It's one thing to be clear, it's another to choose to listen to our own clear message from within. Usually, it's our ego that chooses to ignore it. You must train your ego to realize and respect that you have decided to operate from a place of your own inner power first. The more you seek clarity, the more you will learn how to listen to this expression and guidance of your inner power.

DAILY PRACTICE

» *Work on listening to your intuitive nudges today. Work on asking your intuition if something is a yes or a no and listen to the first immediate feel.*

» *Create a vision board of what you want and where you're going and look at it every day.*

QUOTES

"The hopeful outcome is that we are clear on who we are and what we're about. And we're building things that are sustainable, that are valuable. And, you know, we're able to operate at the outer limits of our ability while we do it. So that was kind of like my process of discovering my why."

—**REID PRIDDY**, OLYMPIC GOLD MEDALIST & AVP CHAMPION

"The present in being present is when your mind and your body are in the same place, doing the one task that you're challenged to do, whether that's having this conversation, or kicking a ball or, you know, dropping in a wave or writing a paper or conversation, whatever it might be, but your mind and your body are together in the same place doing the same thing."

—**DR. MIKE GERVAIS**, SPORTS PSYCHOLOGIST

"So as you get older and evolve further and further, you basically begin to predict the future, because you continually see the future and then build the plan to go out and achieve it."

—**ROB DYRDEK**,
ENTREPRENEUR, HOST OF RIDICULOUSNESS,
HOST OF BUILD WITH ROB PODCAST

"Clarity comes from curiosity, and curiosity is fueled by questions. The more questions we ask, the clearer we get, the much more precise we can be with our message, our mission, and the more fired up and excited we can be about the lives we live."

—**JT DEBOLT**, ENTREPRENEUR & BUSINESS COACH

"Getting really clear on your values and, you got to back it up right, you got to back it up. When you're inspired, you get to back it up when you're not feeling it, and everywhere in between."

—**JOHN MAYER**, 2X WORLD BEACH VOLLEYBALL
TOUR CHAMPION, 4X AVP CHAMPION,
HEAD COACH LMU BEACH VOLLEYBALL TEAM

"Oh, I love the zone. I asked Michael Gervais. That's one of the things I like, how can we get in the zone as athletes; that's all you want to do, is get in the zone and where you feel like you're the games played in slow motion and you can read everything and you know, everything is happening at exactly how you want it to happen. I can definitely identify it. I can't control when it happens. But the more I train and prepare to play like that, the more it happens. So that's one of the reasons why I like training hard because I want to be in the zone where I can just do no wrong or close to that. And that's what is so much fun about being an elite athlete."

—**HOLLY MCPEAK**, OLYMPIC BRONZE MEDALIST,
3X OLYMPIAN, 19X WORLD TOUR CHAMPION,
28X AVP CHAMPION, ENTREPRENEUR, PODCAST HOST

6

Confidence

Self Confidence

I remember the first time I put on the UCLA jersey. I confidently thought to myself, I made it. Now let's go. But I did not feel this confidence every day. There were some days when I questioned if I could compete at this level, especially when new and better athletes would come into the program.

After playing at UCLA, I decided to pursue a career as a pro beach volleyball player. I knew I could play the beach game at a high level, not only because I loved it, but because I felt more confident in myself on the beach court. In 2007 and 2008, Travis Schoonover and I made a run at competing on the AVP qualifier circuit. We trained hard on the court and in the gym as if we had nothing to lose. We had trainers, coaches, and family support. We were a small team in height, but we exuded confidence every time we took the court. In 2008, we qualified for the AVP Hermosa Open.

The day after winning our qualifier bracket, we were matched up against the #1 seeds at the time, Phil Dalhauser and Todd Rogers (who went on to win the Olympic gold medal that year), and despite being the underdog as the #32 seeds (out of 32), we were still confident in each other and in our ability to win. We were confident that we were both going to go out there and do whatever it took to help our team be in a position to win every time we played. While we did not win, we made plays and fought hard, and I'll never forget how fun that match was.

Six years later, Travis and I used that same confidence in ourselves, and we started our company, *West Coast Volleyball Club*, a youth volleyball club in Santa Monica, CA. We wanted to give back to the next generation as well as try to create freedom and abundance for ourselves. We had worked coaching jobs for other clubs but starting our own was daunting. There were a lot of moving parts and many different challenges. Because of the confidence we had in ourselves and in each other, our club is enjoying many years of success, with a growing clientele and a top-notch staff. Our young players strive to be 1% better every day, and learn to accept wins and losses as stepping stones to greater levels of their own personal growth, on and off the court.

You must be confident in yourself at all times. When you are confident in yourself, you exude this energy and others are attracted to it, even your opponents. The more confident you are, the more you will make good decisions and the more productive you will be.

Self-confidence comes from knowing and understanding your sacred 'why'.

Why am I here?

Why do I do what I do?

Why do I want what I want and not want what I don't want?

Who is my tribe?

Once you answer these questions for yourself, your confidence increases. When you exude confidence, you feel supported, since others are drawn towards confident people and energy.

Having confidence in others is huge! People can feel confidence in themselves, and you can feel it when they have confidence in you. It's even more powerful when you share with others how confident you are in them.

No FOPO

Dr. Michael Gervais taught me about NO FOPO—'Fear of Other People's Opinions'. Do not be afraid of what other people may or may not think about you. Especially on social media.

Self-Talk

Self-talk with a champion mindset: Think to yourself; I got this. I am a badass. I can do whatever I set my mind to do. It's all up to me. Even when someone else does something, it's all about how I react. I will stay focused on what I put my mind to. When challenges arise, I will accept them as opportunities to find solutions and to make myself better. I'm having so much fun right now doing what I love to do.

Legendary softball coach Sue Enquist said, "You have a strong and a weak voice every day. We all do. Strong voice says,

'You can do it! You've put in the work! Go for it!'. Weak voice says, 'Nah, you're not ready, you're not that good'. Both those voices will be a part of your life, your entire life. And what separates people that make it to their full potential and those that don't, is they don't let that strong voice always have the last word in your conversation. I'm all about understanding your process, trusting your process, letting the game takeover on gameday. It's ok to have fear, it's not ok to sit in it."

DAILY PRACTICE

» *Use mantras or affirmations to help strengthen your confidence. Repeat to yourself, 'I am confident. I am powerful. I got this. I can do anything I put my mind to. Everything is always working out for me'.*

» *Tell someone in your life that you are confident in them. This could be a friend, a coach, your teammate or a family member.*

QUOTES

"I'm just gonna be me and speak my truth. And that's why I approach a public speaking event to hundreds of people the same way when you show up to a game. You got to say to yourself, I'm just gonna play my game and trust that I have this. I'm not going to think about that technique when I'm moving my foot, I'm just in the game now, I did my hours. I'm trusting I have it in me. And I think that the best way to perform in a moment is to trust yourself."

—**VICTORIA GARRICK**,
FORMER D1 ATHLETE, MENTAL HEALTH ADVOCATE

"When you're able to learn something and do it, well, that gives you confidence when you try something new. I don't know what I'm doing, but I have confidence that I can try to figure it out. And really, that's what it is, because we're not going to do it forever. We're gonna be doing many things."

—**GABBY REECE**, FORMER PRO VOLLEYBALL PLAYER,
MODEL, FITNESS EXPERT, PODCAST HOST

"I feel like there's this confidence that people need in life, self-confidence. It's not cockiness, it's confidence. It's this like a 100% belief in yourself that I'm making it, I'm doing it and nothing is stopping me. And I feel like that comes from moments like that, where you feel like you're a part of something, and it helps you in other areas. I've had to learn how, man I gotta, I gotta have fire, no matter what. But then when you're making mistakes, you can lose that fire real quick. All of a sudden, you're not that cocky and confident, and you make mistakes, right? So how to stay confident in yourself when you're making mistakes is the biggest thing for a young player in any sport."

—**CHRIS "GEETER" MCGEE**, STUDIO HOST FOR
LA LAKERS/GALAXY, 2X EMMY AWARD WINNER

 *"I think you have to be confident, and you have to know how good you are, in order to succeed. But it's like, you don't always have to, you don't have to walk around, like, you're like, the greatest gift to the sport or to the planet. You know, it's the work and the dedication that you've put in, not just what you've been blessed with. But you do have to walk on the court, like, yes, I've put in the time. I deserve to be here. I know. I'm good enough to be here. Yeah, um, it's kind of crazy. Because to actually sit here and think about it, being an athlete has helped me, I think, to be more confident in my personal life."*

—**EMILY STOCKMAN**, AVP CHAMPION

 *"I put in the work. I got to this point. I showed up every day and I practiced. And I'm going to trust that that was enough because I set my intention every day in practice. I trust myself and I trust the skills I've developed to get here. And I don't need to do anything else. And when I've done practice, like, that's how I like to think of the game. I think you inspire yourself in that game because you're like, wow, I made it here. I made it to this game. I went through all those practices month after month. And now I'm here and I'm just going to trust what I'm going to do, what I've always done, and I don't need to be anyone else in myself during the game."*

—**LILY JUSTINE**, 2X NCAA CHAMPION UCLA

CHAPTER 7

Creativity

On the Court as an Athlete

We are creators and we are here to create. Allow yourself to be creative not just artistically, but in all that you do. You know how all spaceships have different names? Imagine that you have the power and curiosity of a spaceship; your own spaceship, and that the energy you have inside you is rocket fuel for your own creativity. It's already in you, your job is to figure out how to use this energy in a creative way.

While there is proper technique in sports, there's not just one way to do something. There are many ways, and it's up to you to figure out your own creativity on technique that you learn. Keywords really help to learn proper techniques.

Learn the game, get inspired by others, but play it in your own way. Learn the techniques, but apply them to the game with your own twist.

On the Court as an Inspired Contributor

You are a creator. When it's time to start the game, CREATE!

Create with your skills, create with your mind, and create with your heart.

When there is low energy, create better energy. When there is winning energy, create more momentum. Do not be afraid to try new ways of doing what you do!!! Everytime you practice your craft, try something new in a way you never thought possible.

Being an inspired contributor means that you are always working to bring something to the table in every situation you experience, which takes creative energy.

Being an inspired contributor means that you are solution oriented and that you are always focused on what it is that you want. It means you are constantly focused on how you can best help your team in every moment.

It's not what you do, but how you do it.

What makes your game different?

How do you keep your game creative and constantly evolving?

Harnessing creative energy is a lot of fun, and provides a good balance in your life, in and out of the game! It allows you to think outside the box.

Allow yourself to be creative in other areas outside of your sport.

Keep it fun!!!

Finding Joy in All You Do

Let your creative juices flow. This is all about allowing! You have creativity inside you, and it's your job to allow it to be evoked! Do not let your own judgments or those of others get in your way of creating. We are here to create.

Become an inspired creator. Create art, businesses, write books, make music—whatever it is that you feel Inspired to create, don't second guess it, just do it, without judgment.

Create for the sake of creating.

Always celebrate others' creativity and never criticize them!

Remember that creativity takes courage, vulnerability, commitment, and authenticity. Even if you 'don't like' a part of someone else's creativity, whether it's in their game or not, always seek to find ways to celebrate it.

The world needs more creativity!!!

The inspired athlete also finds ways to stay creative outside of the game. Finding creative expression outside of the game can really help to keep you inspired when you get back to the game, because it activates other parts of the brain, keeping you fresh. Create art, music, writing, videos, content, buildings, businesses, and most importantly create meaningful relationships. Our minds, hearts and souls are happiest when we are creating all the time.

DAILY PRACTICE

» *Write in your journal, create a video, play music… practice creativity in your own way for at least 10 min every day.*

QUOTES

"This just happens to be by gift. The court is my canvas and I get to create. And maybe it comes a little easier, just because I studied the game for so long. But I always played the, you know, the best I could with what I had at that moment in time. Why? Because there's somebody else out there that would love to trade places with you."

—**MISTY MAY**, 3X OLYMPIC GOLD MEDALIST

"Creativity comes from the soul of what moves you."

—**ANDREW BERNSTEIN**, HALL OF FAME NBA PHOTOGRAPHER, PODCAST HOST

"Creativity is the ability to become so emotionally engaged in what you're doing that, in spite of it fitting the definition of work, it's play. And when you find that sweet spot where suddenly work becomes play, you've found what I believe is your calling. So, if we're to make a few leaps here, to be creative in anything you do is to find your calling."

—**TRAVIS MEWHIRTER**, AVP ATHLETE & SPORTSWRITER, CO-HOST OF SANDCAST PODCAST

"I think when you get in your own way, you can push yourself forward, you can pull yourself back, and I think that has nothing to do with your circumstances, your upbringing, your background, it's very much on you to trust your mind and its creativity to formulate things for you."

—**BRANDIE WILKERSON**, OLYMPIAN, 3X FIVB CHAMPION

"Creativity. I think that kind of stems in with curiosity of, like, we are here to create, and everyone has something to give. Creativity. It can be interpreted in so many different ways. But like, I think we all have that creativity side in us. And it doesn't necessarily have to be like super concrete, whether it's like, beautiful artwork or whatnot. But like, it could be just as simple as, how you make breakfast or how you cook or for me, it could be like, how you play or how you compete. What's your swag?"

—**KELLY REEVES**, AVP PRO PLAYER, NCAA CHAMPION UCLA

AARON WEXLER

Mindfulness

WITH EVERY MOMENT, WE HAVE A CHOICE. WE CAN CHOOSE love or fear. We can choose how we see the world. We can choose our role in the world, our responsibility to ourselves, to the outside world. We can choose how we react at any given moment. We can choose to be a leader or a follower. We can choose to be positive or negative. We can choose love or fear, it's up to us. This is a practice, and the first part of change is awareness.

Becoming Meta-Aware

We must become aware of our thought patterns before we can begin to train our mind to think in a certain way. Become ultra-aware of the tone of your inner voice, so you know when it's really you rather than a projection of you.

This extra awareness of your intuitive nudges is the first part. With practice, we gain ultra awareness of our intuition, and we begin to become aware of our inner voice, and details of our surroundings, within the game as well as in everyday life. Deep breathing, slowing the pace of life, appreciation and gratitude for all things helps increase awareness.

This is called being meta-aware.

Dr. Wayne Dyer was an internationally renowned self-help and spiritual author, as well as a motivational speaker who was a champion of articulating the law of attraction. He once said, "Change your thoughts and change your life." Changing your thoughts is all about training yourself to think differently, to choose to put your focus on certain thoughts. It is my belief that we should put focus on the thoughts that make us feel the best, like:

I got this.
I am powerful.
I am successful.
I am unstoppable.
I am a winner.

After a while your mind will train itself to produce thoughts that are more in line with what you want and what frequency you are generating out to the world.

Mindset Expansion

Incorporate not just new, but *expanded mindsets.* This means that you are able to allow your mindsets to grow and expand as you grow and expand. You can use different specific mindsets depending on your desired outcomes, but the best general mindsets are based on the idea of growth and the idea of being a champion.

This is also about emotional intelligence and emotional control; having the understanding that you are not your emotions, your emotions will come and go, and in fact your emotions are your guidance system.

Growth Mindset

Growth mindset is all about becoming aware of your current thought process, becoming committed to growing as a person, and practicing thinking in a constantly better, more productive way.

Growth mindset is about allowing new, progressive types of thought patterns to grow while letting the 'old school' thought patterns go. Allow the good stuff to expand and let the bad stuff quickly vanish.

Champion Mindset

A Champion mindset is all about deciding to be a champion in your mind before you become a champion in your sport. It's about doing things others aren't willing to do, like putting in the work, showing up even when you're tired, and prioritizing your own dreams first.

A champion mindset is training your mind to stay unconditionally focused on your own actions and your own plan and working that plan how a champion would—with a 100% *all in* type of effort and attitude.

Self-Talk

I ask every guest who comes on my podcast, *Within The Game,* about their self-talk. Legendary Softball Coach for UCLA, Sue Enquist taught me about strong and weak voices. 3 time Olympic Gold medalist as a player and Gold medal winning head coach of the USA women's volleyball team, Karch Kiraly talked about productive and unproductive thoughts. And high level sports psychologist, Dr. Michael Gervais talked about staying productive while mindfully operating in the present with the understanding that there's no such thing as a 'big moment'—there is only the here and now.

It is very important to train your mind to think in terms of positive self-talk to allow you to stay in the here and now. Having better awareness of your self-talk helps you identify when you are in positive self-talk, or our strong voice, and negative self-talk, or our weak voice (productive or unproductive thoughts). Having negative self-talk may seem normal when you hear others speak, but champions do not allow themselves to let other weak voices take over. It's not that we ignore the weak voice, it's that we allow the loudest voice to be our 'strong voice'.

Champion Mindset Mantras

I love what I do and I'm so grateful for my opportunities. I work hard. I love working hard. I'm the best version of myself when I do what I love to do. It feels good to work smart and to work hard. It feels like I'm on my right path when I do my thing. It's not what I do, but how I do it, that makes me stay fired up.

I got this. I'm going to win. I'm a winner. I got this. I know when to make my move to win. I will win. I will always win, because even if I may lose a game or a competition, I will gain a lesson and get stronger. I surround myself with and learn from other winners.

Let's go.

Let's Goooooo!!!!!!!!

Once this skill is practiced and mastered, the next thought pattern of a constantly evolving growth mindset is 'transformative thinking'. This is where we consciously transform old thoughts that might be negative or low frequency, into new, progressive, positive thoughts, instantaneously.

The Peace Sign

Start to become aware of your strong voice as well as your weak voice. There's no one who has done more for me to adopt this concept than legendary UCLA Softball Coach Sue Enquist, who put all of this into the shape of a peace sign, which helps organize the thought patterns in our minds.

Picture this: On the left, put down thoughts that are strong voices. Example: I got this. We're gonna win. I am better than she/he. I remember my training. I am ready. I'm so stoked on this right now! I'm Going to WIN! Let's freaking go!

On the right, put down the thoughts that are weak voices. Example: I can't do this. I'm tired. We're gonna lose. She/he is better than me. I forgot my technique. I don't know if I'm ready for this. I'm going to lose. I don't want to do this. I'm not as good as they are. They're better than me. I'm tired. I'm not supposed to be here.

On the lower left, put everything in your life outside of your game that uplifts you and demands your attention. Example: Family, friends that have your best interests in mind, people that inspire you, school, businesses, goals, dreams, visions, hobbies.

On the lower right, put everything in your life that distracts you from being the best and pulls your energy in the wrong directions. Example: Too much social media, negative people, unfortunate experiences, failures. Look at the whole peace sign. Make peace with all of it. Manage all of it with peaceful ease. All of it. Know that it all has a place and that it's all ok. Become peaceful in your mind, so you can be an excellent manager of your thoughts.

The best way to put into practice the concept of the mind management peace sign is to make the peace sign on a piece of paper and draw big bright arrows from the weak voice side to the strong voice side. Those arrows represent transformative thinking, growth mindset, and growing into being solution-oriented rather than problem-based in your thinking.

Your strong voice is your true voice, and nothing vibrates faster than the truth, so become aware that you can instantaneously transform any weak voice to a strong voice at any given moment and in any situation. This leads to transformative action.

Failure Response System

Sue Enquist taught me about how to create an FRS: A 'Failure Response System' (peace sign)

When you're at practice, create a system that briefly punishes you for allowing your weak voice to take over. Give yourself a break when you find yourself too weak in voice and vocalize it to your coach or training partner. The more aware and accountable you can be of your weak voice, the quicker you can transform it into a strong voice.

AARON WEXLER

DAILY PRACTICE

» *Meditate for 15 min every morning. Quiet your mind and observe your thoughts.*

» *On a daily basis, feed your mind with growth mindset content from people you admire and look up to in areas of your life where you want to get better. Use your free time wisely! Commit to growing personally, spiritually, financially every day. A few of my favorites I listen to on a daily basis for these three categories are Dr. Wayne Dyer, Abraham Hicks, David Meltzer, and Craig Siegel. This can be through books, videos, social media, podcasts, or even in person. This practice is all about preparation; you're preparing yourself now for the best version of yourself later. As Abraham Hicks said, "You're getting ready to be ready." You're slowly drifting towards the best version of your higher self. Your true self. Your connection to your spirit and to source. But you must choose to take the journey of becoming the best version of yourself so that you can stay excited by the journey itself."*

» *Ask yourself, what kind of thought patterns am I experiencing that are not growth mindset? Become aware of every type of thought pattern that you allow yourself to experience. You can then expand on the productive, good feeling thoughts that lead to inspired action and start to let go of other thoughts, the ones that are based in fear or negativity.*

QUOTES

 *"I still have unproductive thoughts as a coach, and I had plenty as a player, and then finally noticing and understanding they're normal, then the third part is just getting myself to a better, to a more productive thought. So, it could be well, I just had a really unproductive thought. All right, I'm going to crush this next serve, I'm going to attack that passer over in zone one, I'm going to hit her in this space between her and the zone one sideline. So those are the main parts noticing. Understanding that they're normal, everybody has them, and then I redirect myself to and put my mind on to a more productive thought or focus."*

—**KARCH KIRALY**, 3X OLYMPIC GOLD MEDALIST,
HEAD COACH OF TEAM USA WOMEN'S VOLLEYBALL,
GOLD MEDAL WINNER, TOKYO OLYMPICS 2020

 *"You know, everybody's got a really good skill, but 90% of your games have to come from your mental side. And so, you know, I truly believe that if you're exercising that muscle and you're really setting your goals to a higher standard, you might not always get them and it's okay to fail. You know, it's not the end of the world, you know, you just want to do better the next time, and nobody's perfect."*

—**ADAM JOHNSON**, 39X AVP CHAMPION, FIVB CHAMPION

 *"I never felt pressure to be a champion, I only felt this urgency to get 1% better, and that's doable. No matter who you are. I don't care if you're a father or grandfather, son or daughter, getting 1% better is manageable in the COVID environment or in a normal society that's thriving and healthy."*

—**SUE ENQUIST**,
11X NATIONAL CHAMPION (SOFTBALL, UCLA)

"Go ahead and do something for someone else. The minute you do something for someone else, you have increased your value. Once you increase your value, you will once again feel as if you are prepared and ready and you  *must make yourself better. Be your own chief betterment officer of your life. Look around you every day and say, 'How can I make her better? How can I make that better? How can I make myself better?' I am the chief betterment officer. It says right here, "get 1% better every day, be the CEO of your life and do it and start it simply by making somebody else's life better."*

—**DAVID MELTZER**, ENTREPRENEUR,
AUTHOR, SPEAKER, HOST OF THE PLAYBOOK PODCAST

"And I believe it all is in the mindset. When you have an elevated state, like you know, when you're those rare days, when you're on fire ten at ten, you can't be stopped no matter what you're doing, whether you're on the basketball court, or  *you're making sales calls, or whatever the case may be, when you're in that elevated state. It's not what can I do, it's what can't I do? And so, it's a mindset. So, what I teach is, I give people the tools to be able to enhance their state and elevate their state on command. And then from that frame, their mindset just sees opportunity and abundance."*

—**CRAIG SIEGEL**, MINDSET COACH, SPEAKER,
HOST OF CULTIVATE LASTING SYMPHONY PODCAST

CHAPTER
9

Bold Action

TAKING ACTION IS THE KEY IN ALL OF THIS!!!

Take bold action. Do the things you know you must do with passion, enthusiasm, and courage.

When I started this project, I knew it was going to be challenging. I didn't know how to write a book or start a podcast. I knew it was going to challenge me in every way—my ability to focus, my attention to detail, my own authenticity and vulnerability, and above all else, my ability to trust the process. I made the decision to write this book, and halfway into the writing process I decided to start my podcast. Both of these action steps were way outside my comfort zone, but I knew what I wanted—to be a published author. I was determined.

Making a Plan

I made a plan with my writing coach, Brian Gruber, and we took off running. We would often meet to talk and check in on the progress of the plan, and he really helped to keep me accountable. The plan for the book was to create an outline, create a writing schedule, and stick to it.

My business partner Travis Schoonover and I work on a plan every day for our business, *West Coast Beach*. We discuss our goals, make and revise plans, and verbally clarify our action steps, helping us stay accountable to each other. This has worked great for us, and is part of our success.

My long-time trainer, chiropractor, and performance coach, Dr. Chad Moreau, always has a workout plan for me to help me achieve my physical goals. These include staying pain free, jumping higher, becoming quicker and ultimately moving better with more efficiency. He is always checking in with me to make sure his plan is perfectly supporting my competition schedule.

Always have a plan for yourself. This is your roadmap, your guide to your goals. The plan can change, or it can be modified based on circumstances, but you must put a plan in place and head in the direction of that plan. This includes setting up your training team: hiring a coach and a trainer, and constantly communicating your plan to both of them so they can best guide you on the action steps you need to take to be successful, and modify when necessary.

The more you commit to your plan, the more you can use emotions and intuitive nudges to feel how that plan is going. A plan and a feel.

Allow Yourself to Go for it

Take More risks!

Sometimes taking bold action means you don't have a plan in place, but you take the action anyway. Many times, this means getting out of your own way and allowing yourself to go for it!

If you get an opportunity to train with someone better than you, take it.

If you get the opportunity to compete somewhere outside your comfort zone, do it.

If you get an opportunity to travel for a competition, go.

Say yes to things that excite you and be courageous in your actions. You will grow more quickly into the best version of yourself when you say yes more often.

Many times, it's the things in life we take risks on that help define us. It's the things that can be uncomfortable—the things outside our comfort zone that are a bit scary.

Stay Courageous

Do not be afraid to fail!!!!

If you allow yourself to go for it and you fail, so what? You can pick yourself up and go for it again, but this time you will be stronger and more equipped with more tools.

I did not finish my collegiate career as a player at UCLA. While I competed for 4 years, I still had 1 more year of eligibility due to redshirting my freshman year. I had been a 'B' indoor volleyball player as a libero, having fallen in love with the beach volleyball game while at Santa Monica High School. Going back and forth from indoor to beach took a toll on my body. By the time I was a senior, I was back in the operating room getting my second knee surgery. One day after practice, I told coach Al Scates that I couldn't continue. It was a combination of frustration for my injury as well as being outplayed by my competition. That same year, UCLA went on to win the NCAA championship and, while I was so stoked for my team and my teammates, I felt like an absolute failure.

It took me some time before I decided to face the coach to apologize for leaving the team, even though my knees were pretty banged up. I remember walking back into coach Scates' office, and with a smile—and a glare from the championship trophy sitting behind him—he said, "Wexler. What brings you in?" With tears in my eyes, I looked right at him and said, "Coach, congratulations on winning the championship. I just wanted to come in and apologize for walking away from the team."

He paused and looked at me with a curious intensity, and told me he appreciated the courage it took for me to come in. It was one of the hardest things I'd ever done, but I also felt good, as I took accountability for my actions.

I was upset with myself for a while over this. But one day, I decided to change the story I had told myself! I may have made a mistake but I could change my story and create a new, more inspired path forward for myself. Two years later, I qualified for my first AVP tournament in Hermosa Beach with Travis Schoonover, an important personal achievement for me. Three years after that, I went back to UCLA and won a National Championship as a volunteer assistant with the women's program under coach Mike Sealy. Five years later, I took a varsity coaching position at Crossroads School, winning the school's first-ever CIF championship, the State

Regional Championship, and made a state finals appearance. I also started my own club *WestCoast Beach* with Travis Schoonover to give back to the next generation of players. And in the past 2 years I have created a podcast, *Within the Game* and wrote this book.

I am not proud of my decision to leave the team and blame it on my knee. I could've stayed with it and I wish I had. It's embarrassing and still difficult for me to write about it and share with others. But the main purpose of me sharing this experience is to inspire someone out there who might be thinking of leaving their team for any reason to just stick with it! If you are thinking about leaving a team for any reason, stick with it! You are surrounded by support! Opportunities to be a part of a team in any capacity are very valuable and precious.

It wasn't bold of me to leave the team, but it was bold to go back and speak with Coach Scates, and it was bold to return to campus and volunteer to work with the next group of athletes, and it was bold to start my own business and it was especially bold to decide to be vulnerable and to share those experiences.

The great football coach Lou Holtz once said, "Life is 10% what happens to you and 90% how you respond to it." Respond to life with bold, inspired action. Do not be afraid to fail, and when you do experience some form of failure, allow it to fuel you for more bold action. You are never a victim. Everything that happens in your life is happening *for* you.

DAILY PRACTICE

» *Take bold, inspired action on something important in your life TODAY that you have been procrastinating on! Whatever this is, it should be a little uncomfortable. Do it today! Right now!!!*

QUOTES

"I set myself daily goals a little literally in a sticky note and then cross out stuff as I slowly but surely accomplish them. It doesn't mean I accomplish every one of them. But I do that every morning, sometimes the night before. So I get up at, you know, at 6 am or 6.30, whenever the sun wakes me up, and I start crossing out those goals."

—**TODD ROGERS**, OLYMPIC GOLD MEDALIST,
3X OLYMPIAN, 52X AVP CHAMPION, 24X FIVB CHAMPION,
HEAD COACH CAL POLY BEACH VOLLEYBALL TEAM

"You know, what inspires me is, competing to be the best Phil Dalhausser. You know, I try. I think a lot of people make a mistake: they compete against the best in their sport or whatever, but they go about it the wrong way. I think Michael Jordan talks a lot about this. He always competed against himself, his best self, while everyone competed against him, and I 100% agree with that."

—**PHIL DALHAUSER**, (AS OF 2022) OLYMPIC GOLD MEDALIST,
4X OLYMPIAN, 59X AVP CHAMPION, 38X FIVB CHAMPION

"I think the purpose and the cause is kind of the end tunnel at the end of the long road. And the mission is kind of the road, right? It's what drives you towards what you're trying to achieve. You know, without a vision or a mission, you either *slow down or you don't really buy into what it is that you're eventually wanting to get out of life, career, family, whatever it is. And so, I would say mission and vision are kind of what is propelling you on that road towards what you eventually want to get out of your life. Yeah, the more succinct and the better, you can buy and engage into your mission, the quicker it is that you're able to go on the road, right?"*

—**RYAN MILLAR**, OLYMPIC GOLD MEDALIST, 3X OLYMPIAN

"If I'm clear on my values, and I can go live it like, it's more about what actions I can take to be the person I want to be on the days that are tough. And so some of my values I thought about, you know, being a lifelong learner. I always want to be  *growing, I always want to be improving. I always want to get better. But most days, I wake up, like, I want to take the easy route, right? I want to do it. I think most of us are drawn to what's comfortable. And so I don't, I don't always feel inspired to do hard things. But because I know that value is so important to me, because I know what the actions are that I have to take to live it. I'm going to do the work and I'm going to do the things that helped me live my values. To me, it's like getting really clear on your values and like you got to back it up right you got to back it up. When you're inspired, you get to back it up when you're not feeling it, and everywhere in between."*

—**JOHN MAYER 2X WORLD TOUR CHAMPION**, 4X AVP CHAMPION, NCAA CHAMPION, HEAD COACH LMU BEACH VOLLEYBALL TEAM

AARON WEXLER

CHAPTER

10

Inspired Living
Living a Life Full of Inspiration

LIVING INSPIRED, MOMENT TO MOMENT, RIGHT HERE AND now, is the ultimate goal!

When we are truly in-spirit, we are inspired, and our thoughts and actions then become inspired. When we operate from inspiration, our actions become strong, great, lasting, and influential. The past becomes less important, and the future remains a projection. We stay in the present moment, we recognize that each moment is a gift, and we act from a place of inspiration and pure potential in all that we do. We choose to be blissful, playful, open, and happy.

Inspired living is feeling the zest for life and allowing that feeling to translate into your craft without judgment. It's about staying authentically honest to yourself, staying vulnerable, staying open minded, and finding joy in all of it.

Living an inspired life is about doing the things that set your soul on fire! It's the things that you do for free because of how those things make you feel.

Whatever gives you the tingles on the back of your neck, follow that.

Whatever makes your true self say yes, since your true self knows exactly what you need at all times, follow that.

Surround yourself with those who help you invoke this feeling of inspired living.

Living an inspired life is about realizing that you are a part of something much bigger than yourself, with the ability to see beauty in the unknown.

It's about making your work internal, being quiet, and allowing your inspirations to come through.

It's about choosing to control your thoughts, emotions, and actions without letting outside forces (people, events or circumstances) have a negative impact on you.

It's about allowing your inner voice and intuitive nudges to become clearer.

It's about operating from this place while you are awake and alive.

It's about getting inspired first, then taking bold inspired action.

It's about practicing this way of living all day long, even when you don't feel inspired.

It's about altruistically lifting someone else up when they are down.

It's about realizing that you are an eternal spiritual being having a human experience and choosing to make this experience the manifestation of your inner vision.

DAILY PRACTICE

» *Create an inspiring morning routine that will help setup your day for an inspired kind of day!*

» *Listen to someone who inspires you today—a podcast, book on tape, or speech on YouTube. Make this a part of your day.*

» *Create a place in your room that you see everyday that reminds you what your ultimate goal is. (For me it's the Pyramid of Inspired Living)*

QUOTES

"Having balance in your entire life system, both in your time, your energy and your mind-share, or your capacity, I think when you're truly living an inspired life. And you get up every day and go from thing to thing to thing that you really enjoy. And you track and prove that joy by the amount of energy you get from it, as opposed to the things that you would do that would draw energy."

—**ROB DYRDEK**, FORMER PRO SKATEBOARDER, ENTREPRENEUR, HOST OF RIDICULOUSNESS & BUILD WITH ROB PODCAST

"Living an inspired life means being able to make a difference. I think every time you wake up, you know, every time you wake up, you should feel inspired, because you have an opportunity to do something. You know, not everybody gets that chance."

—**MISTY MAY-TREANOR**, 3X OLYMPIC GOLD MEDALIST

"Living an inspired life is really looking internal and trying to embody that person that if you were to look around and say, alright, I'm looking for a mentor, someone who embodies all these different qualities, you think of that, but then you start acting that way, you don't need to actually find that person, you need to start acting the way that you want. And I've always tried to surround myself with good people, because if you surround yourself with too many poor character individuals, then they're going to pull you in that direction, where they are. If you're with some really motivating and inspiring people, you're going to, you know, reach new heights. And that's really what it's all about. I've kind of tried to really lead my life as an inspiration, as a mentor, because you just never know who's watching."

—**DAIN BLANTON**, OLYMPIC GOLD MEDALIST, NCAA CHAMPION & HEAD COACH AT USC (BACK TO BACK NCAA CHAMPIONS)

AARON WEXLER

"Understanding and going after your passion, even in the face of hurdles which might mean sleeping on a garage floor, and just staying dedicated over time. And I think periodic reflection; is this the direction I want to continue to go in? I love being involved with a team and in an environment that allows me to learn and grow with others."

—**STEIN METZGER**, NCAA CHAMPION, AVP CHAMPION, OLYMPIAN, AND BACK-TO-BACK NCAA COACH OF THE YEAR UCLA, 2017, 2018

"Living an inspired life is just kind of being like your best version of yourself and identifying who you are. Obviously, that takes time to kind of figure out who you are. I mean, I'm still so young. I feel like I'm at a point, I'm trying to really tap into that, like, what are my core values and trying to live up to those pillars, day in and day out. And I think if you can do that, that's how you find happiness and you hopefully inspire others to inspire yourself to chase your dreams. I think living like knowing who you are, knowing who you are as a person is super important. Yeah, and I live that every day."

—**KELLY REEVES**, NCAA CHAMPION UCLA AND AVP ATHLETE

"And when you have somebody that's living an inspired life, it's not about winning every game, it's not about winning every argument. It's literally having this peace in your heart. Knowing that you're intentional, you're paying attention, you're aware that you're just part of this team, and you live this life authentically, you're gonna have low days, right? But to spark a sense of possibility and inspire others through your positivity is the most powerful gift, you can give somebody this enlightenment that I think is going to be okay. And you do that in your practice arena. That is powerful stuff.

—**SUE ENQUIST**, 11X NATIONAL CHAMPION SOFTBALL COACH, UCLA

 *"I think inspired living is about listening to yourself and doing what feels right in the moment. And that can lead to more inspired moments. And you have to always be ready for the next thing. And I think that staying inspired and being inspired helps so much with that. Because if you're always learning and you don't settle in terms of thinking that you know everything, there's nothing left to learn. Then you can always build on what you already do because you're adding more tools to your toolbox. You know what I mean? And then from there, you can do more things."*

—**GIGI HADID,** FORMER VOLLEYBALL
PLAYER, SUPERMODEL & HUMANITARIAN

 *"Living an inspired life means knowing that you can and will make an impact. And it's, honestly, it's your responsibility to do that. And to feel great about who you are as a person and what your contributions can be, no matter how big or how small, you know, that to me is kind of what it means to live an inspired life."*

—**JT DEBOLT,** BUSINESS COACH & FORMER NAVY PILOT

 *"Inspired living to me is probably pursuing something not only that you're passionate about, but something that you feel called to do."*

—**CAMRYN IRWIN,**
SPORTS BROADCASTER FOR LA RAMS & AVP TOUR

"Having a mindset of inspiration means you wake up every single day, with a purpose. You're living inside your vision, you're inspired, you're motivated, you're driven to conquer your goals, to conquer your moonshots, and to just push forward to make things happen."

—**CRAIG SIEGEL**, MINDSET COACH &
4X MARATHON RUNNER, PODCAST HOST

"Right now, I think living an inspired life means… cultivating relationships, honoring those relationships, but also doing what makes you happy, without sounding too cliché, whatever that means, like being physically active, giving to nonprofits, supporting people who might not be as fortunate as you or me, just doing whatever makes you happy to put yourself in a better position for yourself. That's how you create inspiration for yourself, and also hopefully affect other people, whether they are the closest ones to you, your family, your spouse, your children, or someone you may never see again, it might just be in passing, but you help them or you say something to them, and it makes their day better. I think it's kinda broad, but those are some keys to be inspired by in your day to day, and how you do live an inspired life."

—**MATT PROSSER**, AVP CHAMPION, CANCER SURVIVOR

"You have to be optimistic. You have to have faith. Inspired living to me is connected to faith, which means you have to believe that, well, good things can happen. Because if you believe bad things are going to happen, they probably will. So, I think

there has to be, there has to be some positive. I mean, inspiration is positive. So inspired living is having faith that positive things can happen. And, and, you know, that's about belief."

—**LAIRD HAMILTON**,
LEGENDARY BIG WAVE SURFER & ENTREPRENEUR

Acknowledgements

"Greatness is to inspire the people next to you."
—KOBE BRYANT

Homage and Respect to Kobe Bryant

Kobe was my favorite athlete growing up. The way he competed and trained was purely inspirational. The work ethic he demonstrated was unmatched. The identity of the Black Mamba was fierce, cool, and dominant. The mamba mindset. The way he gave back to his daughters after his playing career was admirable and respectable. The way he articulated himself off the court was impressive. The way he continued to express his creativity through his movies, books, and businesses was motivating.

In the middle of my process creating this book, Kobe along with his daughter Gigi as well as seven other souls passed on from this life in a tragic helicopter accident. This event not only shook me, but the whole world. It made all of us realize how precious life is—how special each moment we get to experience as athletes both in training and in competition really is. It brought the athletic world together, and I know Kobe will always be remembered for inspiring others.

For the interview section of this project, I had a list of people I intended to interview, people who I thought were living their versions of their inspired life. Kobe was #1 on that list. This project is in honor of Kobe, his family, and everyone who he inspired and continues to inspire.

Tribute to Mom & Dad

My dad was at every one of my sporting events for as long as I can remember. He was always there, quietly observing from the stands, always engaged in the situation. He worked hard to help turn my athletic goals into realities, from playing catch in the front yard, to hiring coaches, to installing a basketball rim on the garage, to spending countless hours late at night at the baseball field, to introducing me to yoga when I was 12 years old and going to practice at 7am before school, to waking up at 5am for long drives and long days at volleyball tournaments. He sacrificed much of his own free time for me. He saw a lot of my plays in many sports; some good, some not so good, and while he had constructive criticism, it always felt like unconditional love and support. You were there for it all, Dad, and not only were you there, you never complained about anything, you had fun with it all, and you were engaged in my personal and my team's success. I appreciate you and love you so much for that.

The Love
Car Wash

One day, when I was a kid, my mom took me to a car wash, and I remember standing there as the cars went through thinking to myself, there should be a "love" car wash; where all the people that are going through a tough time would enter and get all loved up; when they emerged on the other side, they would be transformed into the most loving, most inspired versions of themselves. You would walk on one end full of hate, confusion, desperation. Perhaps you forgot who you truly are, and you would enter and get loved up and inspired and come out the other end surrounded by new-found love, light, and joy. What happens in the tunnel of the car wash is really a process of going inside and discovering my true power and how to activate it. I told my mom that I thought there should be this love car wash accessible to everyone. This book is my 'love car wash'. Thank you, mom, for always encouraging me and inspiring me to allow myself to go for it.

My
Writing
Coach

Thank you to Brian Gruber, my writing coach who I met in Thailand at an ashram. After taking his creative writing workshop, we started working together on this project and he helped me shape the vision for this project, offered precious guidance, and pushed me to completion. He was with me every step of the way and I am forever grateful to you! Thank you dear friend.

Paying it Forward

When you have realized that it's all about living inspired, in whatever way you define it, help others by paying this message forward. Remind your loved ones that they can achieve Inspired Living too, and that's it's a choice.

Pay this message forward most importantly with your actions, and others will see it and sense it.

CONTRIBUTIONS

Special THANK YOU to all of the contributions to this project made by the following amazing people:

Dain Blanton Olympic Gold Medalist

Eric Fonoimoana Olympic Gold Medalist

Todd Rodgers Olympic Gold Medalist

Karch Kiraly 3x Olympic Gold Medalist

Reid Priddy Olympic Gold Medalist

Phil Dalhausser Olympic Gold Medalist

Rich Lambourne Olympic Gold Medalist

Ryan Millar Olympic Gold Medalist

Misty May-Treanor 3x Olympic Gold Medalist

Kerri Walsh Jennings 3x Olympic Gold Medalist

Rob Dyrdek, Former Pro Skateboarder, Host of Ridiculousness, Entrepreneur, Host of Build With Rob Podcast

Laird Hamilton, Legendary Big Wave Surfer

Gabby Reece, Former Pro Beach Volleyball Player, Fitness Expert, Podcast Host

Gigi Hadid, Supermodel & Former Volleyball Player

Chris "Geeter" McGee, 2X Emmy Award Winner, Studio Anchor/Host for LA Lakers

Dr. Mike Gervais, Sports Psychologist & Podcast Host

Sue Enquist 11x NCAA Champion UCLA Softball

Kenny Lofton, Legendary Pro Baseball Player, Entrepreneur

David Meltzer, Former Sports Agent, Entrepreneur, Author, Speaker

Craig Siegel, Mindset Coach, 4x Marathoner, Entrepreneur, Podcast Host

Timothy Schultz, Powerball Winner, Podcast Host

Lily Justine, 2x NCAA Champion, UCLA

Victoria Garrick, Mental Health Advocate and former D1 Athlete

John Hyden, Olympian & Legendary AVP Champion

Casey Patterson, Olympian & AVP Champion

Adam Johnson, Legendary AVP Champion

Holly McPeak Olympian, Coach, Entrepreneur

Stein Metzger, Olympian & NCAA 2x Coach of the Year

Matt Prosser, AVP Champion & Cancer Survivor

Nick Lucena (zoom), Olympian & AVP Champion

Tri Bourne, Olympian, AVP Champion, Podcast Host

Torino Johnson, Basketball Coach, CSLA

Mark Ozello, Coach & Mentor

Mari Jo Deutschman, Coach & Mentor

Reo Sorrentino, Coach & Mentor

Kelly Reeves, NCAA Champion

Travis Mewhirter, Author & Pro Athlete

Anthony Davis, State Champion Basketball Coach, Crossroads

Brandie Wilkerson, Olympian & AVP Pro

Prince Daniels Jr. , Author & Former NFL Running Back

Garry Gilliam, Entrepreneur & Former NFL Player

Camiryn Irwin, Sportscaster, Host of LA Rams

Emily Stockman, Pro Beach Volleyball Player & AVP Champion

John Mayer, AVP Champion, Head Beach Volleyball Coach LMU, Podcast Host

JT DeBolt, Entrepreneur & Leadership Coach

Reo Sorrentino, PE Teacher, Friend, & Mentor

Clayton Joseph Scott, Musician, Friend, Yoga Teacher

Javis Huggins (J Brave), Musician, Friend, Visionary

Made in the USA
Las Vegas, NV
20 October 2022